I0568240

SKIVING DOWN THE BONES

Poems by

Olive L. Sullivan

Meadowlark
PRESS
Emporia, Kansas, USA

Meadowlark Press, LLC
meadowlarkbookstore.com

Meadowlark Poetry Press
meadowlarkpoetrypress.com
P.O. Box 333, Emporia, KS 66801

POETRY / Subjects & Themes / Death, Grief, Loss
POETRY / Women Authors
POETRY / American / General

ISBN: 978-1-956578-31-7

Library of Congress Control Number: 2022949993

In memory of my beloved husband,
Stephen A. Harmon

Author's Note

Long before the Pandemic locked us all into our homes, my personal period of isolation began with my 2017 diagnosis of Acute Myleoid Leukemia, a particularly deadly and fast-acting cancer. I spent close to three months in one room of a locked isolation ward at the hospital. All visitors had to pass through an airlock. Chemo had stripped my immune system and left me a frail version of my usual self. Then I spent another three months living in an apartment near The University of Kansas Medical Center in Kansas City while my parents cared for me and my husband commuted back and forth from our small town two hours south. My dad was just beginning to show serious signs of the Alzheimer's disease that would leave him with no memory of these events, not even the memory of me as his daughter. His story is also part of this volume. My first book of poetry came out while I was undergoing chemo. I also used the time to work on my bookbinding apprenticeship, which is where the title of this collection comes from. Skiving is the paring of leather at the edges so it is easily folded over the book's cover boards.

Next, my kidneys failed. I dropped down to 80 pounds. I could see death on the edges of my vision. In November of 2018, I started dialysis. In December of 2020, my husband died of Covid-related pneumonia. I was in limbo, unable to care completely for myself, but left with a house, a big dog, responsibilities, and a fledgling bookbinding business. My dear friend Amy Nixon came to live with me, and I at last got a kidney transplant on May 14, 2021. It's bittersweet; I am alive, but so many others are not. My husband, who fought so hard to keep me alive, is not here to share my joy and resume our life of travel. We had such plans! And my father died, at age 90, in August of 2021.

The worst irony of it all is that for me to live, someone else had to die. I am eternally grateful for the family who donated their loved one's kidneys to me and another patient on the transplant list. I urge you all to consider becoming living kidney donors. There are some 90,000 Americans awaiting transplant right now, and of course many more worldwide. For more information, please visit the website at Big Ask/Big Give. If becoming a living donor is not the right choice for you, please fill out the organ donor information on your driver's license.

The poems in this volume tell about my descent into darkness, the collateral damage to my family and friends that occurred over the five (and counting) years I have been struggling with my health, and my return to the light, changed, but still standing. There are also other true stories of loss and grief and return to light in this book.

I dedicate this volume to the organ donors and their families, to the nurses and doctors, and to all those grieving and struggling in what we hopefully call the post-Covid world.

Poems

I.   Descent into Darkness

II.   Hard Love

III. Recognition

IV. Return

Descent Into Darkness

Invocation to Breede

I dedicate this fire of my bones
to holy Breede,
patroness of poets,
goddess of creative flame,
honored with fire.
I create this altar
of sycamore and oak
stacked precisely in overlapping squares.
I start the flame
with poem in praise of her,
touched with a long wooden kitchen match,
for she is also goddess
of the hearth,
the heart of the home.
I throw in my beautiful hair,
loosened by the poisons
they pumped through my body
to save it,
my blood boiling like lava,
platelets and leukocytes
fleeing like scared refugees
to a farther shore.

I have been sleeping
in a fetal curl,
hugging myself,
seeking warmth, containment, safety.
In the light of this holy fire,
I open my arms wide,
fling my sorrows into the heart
of the flame,
sear my open hands
with remembering,

let my tears dissolve
my damaged skin like ash.
I dedicate this bonfire of my bones
to holy Breede,
patroness of poets,
goddess of creative flame.
Let be what thou wilt,
oh holy Breede.
Let all else burn.

Luminous

The rough patina of my skin
dissolves into the sky like
a river of tiny blue butterflies,
like flakes of ash, like embers.
As I hold up my arms,
I see my own bones, translucent,
glowing with a silvery light,
reaching towards the sun.
I step through the Lion's Gateway—
am transformed to light,
back to the essence of stardust
from which we are made.
Don't cry for me.
Don't cry for me.
I am
luminous.
Oh,
luminous.

The Winter Aspect

In spring, we blessed the house
with bundles of honeysuckle and lilac,
in the summer with daylilies, roses.
In fall, we gathered bur acorns
and sycamore branches,
laid oak logs on the hearth
against the coming darkness.

At first in winter we gathered pine cones
and fir boughs,
lit colored lights, strung tinsel,
sang.
But in January,
the neighborhood's a columbarium,
the sky ashen with gray clouds
that smell like snow
but deliver only ice,
sunrise, glittering, brittle as bone,
the ice a hard shell encasing woe.

We burrow down,
fold inward, brush the ash away,
cradle our bones, seared by chemicals,
scarred by the knife marks
of the goddess' winter aspect,
the marrow boiling like lava,
transforming the foundation of the self—
our blood type altered:
Dogs that, in summer, smiled and waggled a greeting
now curl their lips, snarl as if at a stranger.
Children bury their faces in their mother's shirts.

The queen of winter, bitter, laughs,
spreads out her arms,
demands a sacrifice.
Onto the pyre
we throw unfinished craft projects,
our mismatched china,
our too-small clothes that will fit if only we lose ten
pounds—
things we have been unable to let go.
She demands more,
things that matter,
memory, a hank of hair,
a rag, our very bones.
We add a prayer to keep our hearth fires lit.
We damp our outrageous dreams like coals in ash.
Maybe we will dare to act on them in spring,
if spring will only come.
If we are still here to greet it.

There are no stars tonight, no waxing moon.
The vixen screams. The hunting owl calls.
All else is silence

We hunker down, cradle our scarred bones,
hold hands under the blankets piled on the bed.
We close our eyes and dream in color—
honeysuckle, lilac, the return of the sun.

Homecoming

I've dreamed this life once before—
the easy, slow passage of days,
bright faces gathered round a dinner table,
hard work, cool at night. But
that time there wasn't this
exhaustion, this urge to sleep forever and
forever. That time everyone was
young and dreaming of tomorrow.

Portents

The sky tonight
is white and black.
Latticed by the oak tree branches,
it pushes down,
oppresses, like
the blank moment after you wake
from anesthesia wondering
who you are, where, and
what's happened to you.
Under the white night sky,
the shadow of a fox
slips between the oak tree
and the car in the driveway, leaving
an invisible trail
that might draw
darker shadows after it.
Far away, a family sits down to dinner,
someone laughs at a bad sitcom,
someone reaches for her lover's hand,
somewhere,
a newborn baby's mother cries.

Melon Time

My hands smell like cantaloupe,
sweet, musky and sticky,
even though I've washed them twice.
And the scent takes me back to
the solid chunk of the knife
through pale orange flesh
onto my oak chopping block,
the precision of four neat crescents
from each pregnant half, the simple
geometry of half-moons notched and
sliced into the big blue bowl,
the meditative art of daily life
so hard to find: the rhythm,
color, flash of blade through flesh,
and the emptiness of pale green rind
like all my empty days.

Oblivion Tango

Guitar and piano
whisper in the corner,
lonely as layers of dust.

My calluses have softened,
cradled in your palm.

You are the fixed foot,
the steadfast sun at the center
of my wayward orbit,
but the moon
still circles me alone.

I pluck the guitar,
pick notes falling
into a minor chord.

My fingertips
start to bleed.

Summer

It's 3 a.m. and Bruno's up on the garage roof
wailing the blues while
down in the front yard
Shakespeare's going crazy
'cause he can't see who's up there with the cat.
And heat presses down
like an iron on damp washing—
Bruno's mournful howl,
the flash of sheet lightning and
the prayer for rain,
a flood of frogs and peepers
crossing the grass
like the next bitter plague.

Sunday Morning after Church

The maize-colored carpet
itches against my face
where I snooze on the hearth,
a dachshund pressed along my spine.

Sound falls onto me in layers:
Dad's music on the stereo,
the gentle clanking from the kitchen,
the crackle of the fire,
the warm breath of the dachshund,
my own slow heartbeat
picking up the vibration of the earth
beneath the floor.
I am floating on a sea of sound,
a blue-green sea that rocks me,
melting me.

I dream of angels singing Christmas hymns,
of dogs romping in the snow,
of gingerbread.
I never dream of brimstone.

I never thought then of
the anger that now knots my spine
and locks my jaw, pushing my shoulders
into the base of my skull,
years and years of it, locked away.

Why can't I remember only the itchy maize carpet,
the music, the dachshund,
the bliss of the blue-green sea?

Upon Listening to Mahler's Symphony #4 in G Major

St. Ursula stands by laughing—
well, she's not really laughing,
more of a smile, a smirk,
wry, crooked half smile,
as if she's thinking how foolish we all are
and trying not to show it.
Is it not a scream instead?

Isn't she the saint
who carried her severed breasts on a platter
like two great pink Jell-O molds?
No—that's Barbara.
Ursula is the one pierced by arrows
like a pincushion, a demure hedgehog.
Isn't she the patron saint of dance?
Of fits of giggles at the dinner table?

She's the patron saint of archers.
Her saint's day is my birthday.
She is the patron of female students,
maybe studious, pale girls like the ones
who followed her from Great Britain
to their deaths. Maybe they were dancing instead?

Does her breath smell of honeysuckle?
Have I read she's beloved of bees,
with her lips open to receive the queen
or the wild rose blossom?

She stands, smiling. She knows
what we already know.
It's just that she is willing
to say it out loud,
and be pierced for it.

Drought

Three long months without a drop of rain
and the ghost of corn rattles its bones in the moonlit fields,
the brittle grass whispers its own soft name,
the tang of dust covers roads, windowsills,
the wings of prairie birds in flight.
The only relief comes late, late at night.

Relief comes at last late, late at night.
As morphine takes away deep pain, a gentle rain
can be the tender hand that wipes
dust and tears from tiny faces, fields
fears, quenches fires, puts flowers on the windowsills,
whispers in the darkness your own familiar name.

The brittle grass whispers its own name
to calm itself late, late at night
when it's grown so tall it peeps over the windowsills,
spreads over new-plowed garden beds, rain
causing it to run amok in imaginary fields,
but at arid dawn, all dreams of wild growth take flight.

The wings of prairie birds in flight
brush the dry burned brown silk of the corn, name
the ghost of lost crops rattling their bones afield,
waiting, waiting, then folding wings at evening light
bowing their heads, dreaming of rain—
the prairie birds—meadowlark, killdeer, whip-poor-will.

The tang of dust covers the roads, the windowsills,
and the farmer's wife dreams of taking a flight
some far place where long-forgotten rain
caresses her dry skin, whispers her secret name,
holds her through the misty night,
drowns, washes out the ghosts of barren fields.

The ghost of corn rattles its bones in the moonlit fields,
and the farmer's wife leans over her dusty windowsill
seeking the scent of rain late, late at night,
hoping sheet lightning zaps the moon in flight,
praying that God will save this harvest-only-in-name
by opening the floodgates and releasing rain.

Birds in flight call out her name,
harbingers of the longed-for rain; the rattling corn fields
late, late at night still haunt her dusty windowsills.

The Angler's Rest

For the great Gaels of Ireland
are the men that God made mad,
for all their wars are merry,
and all their songs are sad.
—G.K. Chesterton

In the Angler's Rest in Ballina,
Pius Powers tunes his violin
and draws the bow across the strings.
It sobs beneath his gnarled hands,
keening the misery of generations,
cutting through chatter and laughter
and the fug of cigarette smoke
to the listening center.
Gi' us a song, then, Pius,
comes the cry, *Tell us a story.*
The violin's voice deepens for an instant,
then squawks exuberantly as
Pius rolls into "The Rocky Road to Dublin."

The room explodes into a thumping swirl
of dancing bodies taken over by
the dreams of the violin.
From the hill above the town, where two lovers argue,
the pub near the pier
is a beacon of light
on a backdrop of black ocean and stars,
the night shivering with music,
the hills settling in deep to listen,
and the violin's full sorrow
gives way—though its sobs
still underlay the raucous joy—
to its younger self—the violin
and Pius Powers remembering when
it used to be a fiddle.

Waiting for the Dead

Paris, City of Light,
is also a city
that remembers the dead.
From the veterans who march
to the Arc de Triomphe
to the catacombs,
the city—
like all cities—
is built on bones.
The dead wait for us
even as we wait for those
who keep us frozen
like the marble owl
on the unmarked tomb
of the founder
of the Paris *Herald*.

The dead wait for us,
like the vampire of French folklore,
like Lison, the werewolf god
of the Guarani,
like Baron Samedi,
who dances among the vaults
and mausoleums of New Orleans,
like those who celebrate
el Dia de los Muertes
with picnics in *el cemetario*,
sharing the news
with those long gone.

I knew a woman once
who waited for her mother to die
before having children of her own.

She said
she didn't want her mother to know
she'd had sex—
even though she was married,
happily—
at least we think so.

My grandmother never talked
about her little sister.
I was so ashamed,
is the only thing she ever said,
but family gossip left
enticing clues and rumors—
scandal, sex, disgrace,
inflamed
my writer's imagination.
I knew I could not
tell the story
while Grandma
was alive to read it.

I'm not the only one
waiting for the dead
so I can come to life—
a man I know
kept his hair cut short
until his mother died,
then grew it hippie long.
He only cut it later,
because, he said,
he'd realized
the 60s were dead too.

We wait for the dead
to let go
their bony grasp on us
so we, unfrozen,
can soar free,
to be who
we are meant to be—
but even as we rise,
gravity links hands with
the werewolf and the Baron,
the catacombs and the grave,
to pull us home
where the dead wait for us.

Snapshot

Someone in this wedding snapshot won't be here next year.
The photographer snaps the shutter and we start
at the sudden blinding flash. The bride turns her face away in tears.
Will it be her grandfather, a man well on in years,
who fades from this captured image, but not from our lonely hearts?
Someone in the wedding snapshot won't be here next year.
Perhaps the brittle alcoholic wife who buries woes in beer
while her stoic husband practices a subtle art,
denying trouble even as his wife dissolves in drunken tears?
Perhaps the next familiar face to disappear
will be that bleak young man, set by his misery apart—
Someone in this wedding snapshot won't be here next year.
Maybe the one to leave won't in sorrow disappear—
the bridesmaid on the left, you see, is poised for a fresh start—
her blinding smile hiding a belly-fluttering fear
as she pictures her new life, a change of gears
from small-town life to a city chic and smart.
Someone in this wedding snapshot won't be here next year.
I search each face for clues, blink, and release my heavy tears.

Marais des Cygnes

That night we drove back from the doctor's in Kansas City,
I wrote a poem.
As we crossed the Marais des Cygnes river,
my words spilled out,
celebrating the darkness,
the call of spring peepers,
the night heron,
the splash of a beaver,
the muttering ducks settling in for the night,
and the call of a late flock of geese coming into the marsh.

You asked how I could hear all that
over the sound of the road and the radio,
and I said I just knew it was there,
the way I can feel the Rockies
pulling me westward,
orienting me to my place on earth.

I wrote on a scrap of paper,
or maybe in my blue notebook.
I don't know.
That poem is lost.
I searched all my journals,
scraps of paper spilling over the kitchen table
waiting for me to do my taxes,
backs of envelopes,
the recesses of my cluttered mind.

I believe that poem was magic good,
but it is lost,
as are you, my love,
and the magic.

Closing Time

From behind the lens
the world seems brighter,
more real, but harder to touch.
When you put the camera down,
you find yourself in black and white,
the magic of the studio
just so many paper backdrops,
the bright sunlight
a series of lamps too hot to touch.

Pick up the guitar
and pluck the strings,
but when the audience leaves,
the musician hears only the silence,
becomes a hollow echo in the backstage dark.

When the music stops,
when the spotlights go out,
when the photographer packs his equipment,
when the musician closes his guitar case,
the man with the hole in the center of his heart
turns off the light.

Inheritance

My mother says
the best inheritance
she ever got
was a case of Hershey's syrup
and a secondhand collie dog
left to her by her brother.

The syrup was an artifact
of their childhood,
when everybody got
a dish of vanilla ice cream,
homemade, every night.

The dog was supposed to be
on her last legs.
She lived another fifteen years.
My mother is good
at keeping things alive.
She is good at survival.

She doesn't talk about
her other inheritance,
the fear of dying of a stroke—
or rather, not dying of it.
Her brother's aneurysm
took him fast—
still counting on that
evening dish of ice cream,
on herding sheep with that collie.

My mother fears being trapped inside
her useless body—
which has always been so useful,

so obedient to her commands.
She is one of those women
who can't sit still,
who is always doing.
She fears the drooping eyelid,
the slurred speech.

She'd rather go quick—
if she has to go at all—
get it over with,
eat ice cream in the afterlife.

Hard
Love

Something More

I can feel you coming up the stairs like
a current underneath the soles of my boots,
electric from the earth, vibrating
through concrete and carpet and steel,
and when you walk through the door
sparks snap between our eyes
and fingertips, my hair rises
like a halo glowing with the static
of intense desire and
I can almost feel the hiss of
your palm along my naked skin,
the taste of your curious mouth on mine—

But you are not for me.
My muse, she is the jealous kind,
grips my shoulder and whispers
thunder in the pit of my soul,
Channel passion into words,
don't waste it on hopeless desire.
She comes to me like angels who must say
fear not, I bring you greatness
and joy—but, oh, sometimes I long
for the touch and taste, the spark
of human love, not empty
breath of language hissing along the ages.

Rear View

I see a woman driving down the road in a red car—
she's wearing sunglasses and tears track down her cheeks.
I see her in my rear view mirror
and I know she thinks her heart is breaking—
she thinks she understands sorrow.
She thinks she knows about grief.
She doesn't know that each new injury
layers onto the last like grains building up and up
into a miles-long sandstone mesa,
each weighing down
on the one before until the whole is solid rock.

She's driving down the road in a red car
and her glasses are mirrors that hide her eyes,
hide her so she doesn't have to see
the miles stretching out before her.
She looks back and I see her crying

from the inside out, I see her
in the rear view mirror from
behind mirrored glasses.
She thinks she understands grief.
She thinks she knows about sorrow.
I barely recognize her now.

Bitter Salt

I'll lie here and drink salt,
bitter, bitter, bitter
rivers of salt lying in my belly like
bitter earth.
Oceans of salt—from where? I
thought all of sorrow's oceans
had gone dry—yet
now it seems they'd just gone underground—
bitter, black, hidden rivers that
upon the first crack in the arid earth
burst forth like geysers
burning, bitter, steam and sorrow,
where only yesterday
the world was covered with
bright, dancing yellow flowers
and foxtails brushed
the face of the glorious sun.

Christmas Eve

Grief grips my gut,
to see her still struggling
to speak clearly,
still halting in her gait.
How I'd hoped—
The doctors say she'll outgrow it,
but her new sister shines,
a gleeful bud of perfection.
How will they cope?
What will they lose, or gain?

My secret sin is petty disappointment—
the longing for a perfected reflection.
How can I have a granddaughter
to whom words are hardship
and frustration?
My childhood disgust
at a palsied cousin
lurks in the back of my tight skull,
unspoken, so bitter
I cannot say it aloud to anyone.

On Christmas Eve,
she joins the children's sermon,
hugs each child there, completely fearless.
When the choir sings,
she lifts her palms
in an attitude of blessing,
and when we light the Christmas candles,
her face glows with its own radiance.
My cold heart cracks—
She cannot speak, my granddaughter,
but she can see.

Witness

Walking past the clangorous rows of slot machines,
we tuck our heads, hunch our shoulders—
it's like walking through a gauntlet, assaulted by sound,
by seizure-triggering lights and flashes.
Gambling is not why we came here.
What we find in Las Vegas is not
its glittering lights or contortionists and pop stars,
but a well of grief so deep you could dive in
and discover bioluminescent creatures at the bottom.
If there is a bottom.

My granddaughter, damaged, traumatized,
looks at me only from the corner of her eyes.
If she catches me looking at her,
she buries her face in her mother's shoulder. Sometimes,
she sidles toward me, but
she is like a cloud shadow on the desert;
if I look too quickly, she is gone.

Oh, she is gone, gone,
my Las Vegas granddaughter.
I offer her the pink bunny I brought from Kansas.
She clutches her mother, buries her face,
so like my mother's face, so like my own.

She is lost to me,
distance only a tiny factor in our family tragedy,
the one triggered when her father
couldn't control his narcissistic rage,
when he made the choice to carry a gun,
when he took that shot she witnessed,
when he made her into a victim,
lost me my son—her father—
eighteen years in prison for a split second choice.

I won't see him again.
The cancer was already creeping through my bones
last time I saw them as a family, my smile, his smile,
my granddaughter's bright grin.
He won't see his daughter again.
She won't look at me. I can't
look away.
I can't touch the bottom of this sorrow.

Love's Like That

When I fell in love with him, the apple
did it. It was the way he sliced it, round
and ordinary, yet crosswise, the dappled
stem end left intact, pale circles with round
center seeds a star of arsenic, like fish,
tainted, gleaming to the eye with the smell
of death within. Love's like that. The blue dish
was offered; I bit a slice and the spell
was cast. No warning thunder shook the sky,
no portentous omens shook the ink pen
in my hand, and I didn't then catch the lie
lurking in his velvet eyes, but that's when
I fell. Loving him was like a pyramid
falling point down on my chest. But I did.

Coming To

And it seems there's nothing for it but to
sink down and down and down
until you're cradled forever in Gaia's stony arms,
nothing for it but to let go and fall.
You can't even remember what happened
to the month of March, here it is April and
the tulips you planted last fall in hope
of happiness, they're blooming now by
the cracked doorstep and they are all
the color of broken hearts and bruises,
broken stems oozing green sap and ragged-edged leaves
bent backward way too far and
all you do is work and sleep and everything else is
the sound of brain-damaged freaks huffing
paint thinner in the basement, the smell of
cigarettes and gin and the sour smell of misery and
there is no way out but to let go and fall,
and then you open your eyes and
over you his face is twisted into a parody of
love or something you mistook for love and
the stick of firewood he holds in his hands like
a baseball bat, as if your face were the home run,
the crack of your cheekbones the cheer of the crowd—
the World Series of Misery, and
afterwards you can never remember if
the crack was the sound of the stick breaking in two, half
flying off the bed and him grabbing another one and saying
Move your hands, bitch, I'm gonna hit you again, and
you touch your face and find it swollen and
unrecognizable and the color of broken tulips by
the crooked steps and your hand comes away red and
months later when you can't even remember the weeks between
April 19 and August you still can feel the lump beside your eye,

still feel the crack inside your skull, the splinter
of pain into your left eye and down your jaw and
coming out your mouth as a primal scream of hatred as
you run, you know you're bleeding
like those tulips your bare feet crush as you fly down
the broken concrete steps and there's nowhere left to go
but to let go and fall and so you do, let go, and
fall powerless powerless powerless but
suddenly you feel yourself caught up, borne by a net
woven by the hands of those who've always loved you,
watched you fight your way through days of agony and
waited for you to let go so they could catch you and
you are cradled in your mother's arm and you say
I wish I'd known you'd be here when I fell and she says
you must think all I care about is money and you say, *well, yeah,*
and then you let yourself be cradled by your mother's arms
and she says *you are my baby and I'm glad you're here,*
and somehow you find yourself sitting at the dining table
inhaling the scent of baking bread and sawdust and
wondering why you hadn't know the nightmare
couldn't end until you were ready to wake up, and now
the figure of a man limps through your dreams, his face
a mask of rage
because you're safe, you're back inside your own sweet skin and
there's no way he can touch you now.

Road Trip

And for myself,
a small blue star on the inside of my thigh,
a black bear on my left wrist.
an Oldsmobile full of dogs
and summer sweat, the ocean behind us and
thieves and liars on the road ahead,
their unseeing eyes
ignoring to their sorrow
the curses blossoming beneath
my sacred skin.

Unhooked

—You fit into me
like a hook into an eye

a fish hook
an open eye.
                —Margaret Atwood

It's like being yanked all
glistening and wet to thrash
and flail in too-bright airless sunlight—

It's like having the barbed hook ripped
from your bleeding jaw,
gills pumping frantically for cool wet breath—

And it's like slipping from the foreign hand,
the icy shock as current pulls you in,
then swimming down the brown cool stream
like nothing's happened—

A Woman is Walking

A woman is walking into the woods.
She is wearing a red coat.
Her name is Alice.

Her name is Alice.
She is walking in the woods.
She is searching for something
but she cannot remember what it is.

She cannot remember what it is
but she knows it's something important—
her mother's recipe for cornbread, maybe,
or the baby's medicine.

The baby's medicine? That
can't be right? What baby?
She doesn't remember the baby,
who is now forty-seven.
But there is a rattle in the pocket of her red coat.

There is a rattle in the pocket of her red coat.
Her feet rustle through layers of fall leaves.
She thinks she sees a deer, or a child playing.
She goes deeper into the woods.

She goes deeper into the woods.
She is wearing a red coat.
She is searching for something she's forgotten.
Her name is Alice.

She goes deeper into the woods.
Her name is Alice.
She can't remember.

Turquoise Ring

Native Americans use turquoise as a powerful healing tool connecting heaven and earth. It is associated with personal protection.

This is all about forgetting,
but in my dreams, he is remembering.
In my dream, he says,
I guess I'll never wear that turquoise ring again.
I don't even know where it is.
—You gave it to me a few years ago, I say.
Remember?
He doesn't. *Did you ever get it fixed?*
—Yes, I used to wear it all the time,
like you.
It's too big now, or maybe I am too small.

The dream follows me all day.
My dad doesn't remember who I am.
I search my jewelry stash for the ring.
Late that night, under the waxing crescent moon,
I drive to my parents' house.
I creep through the front door,
creep down the dark hallway,
creep into their bedroom.
Kneeling by the bed,
I slip the turquoise ring
under Dad's side of the mattress.
I creep into his dreams.
I whisper, *Remember. Please remember.*

Comancheria

For Steve

There's still snow on the peaks
of the Sandia Mountains
when we drive through Tijeras Canyon at dusk.
Sunset splays itself across the city
as we cross the Rio Grande.

Morning finds us in another country—
no more West Texas wasteland.
West Texas, you could be on the moon.
New Mexico, there is still snow on the peaks.
The road signs are in Navajo.
The woman at the quick mart smiles.
She tells me there are petroglyphs nearby.
There are always petroglyphs nearby.
What I want is silver squash blossom earrings.
She shakes her head—
No, just this—
the glass counter full of pawn jewelry.
She smiles. I
smile. A sign. We drive on.

The signs are in the rock faces
of the mesas, the Palisades, the low hills
that made good cover for the Comanche raiders,
their sturdy Andalusian horses an accidental gift
from the Spanish
who finally retreated south,
drew a line, said, *This is Mexico.*
That is the Comancheria.

The rock face slides down,
collecting a scree of secrets.
The signs are everywhere.
We don't know how to read them.

The Woman Now

The man who has always been
strong, who has supported his woman
in her pain and fear, lies now
in a hospital bed, weeping.
He weeps for the self he's lost,
the inner man he never had the chance
to be. And the woman sits and
holds his hand.

And here is the good daughter
coming to sit at her side.
She has her own babies and
her own hard work and Tom,
and yet as ever she is there
to hold her mother's hand,
to bless her father, weeping.

But the woman who now looks up
is not weak or afraid.
She reaches out her knotted hand,
looks at the dying man and says,
It's all right. Go on home.
We'll manage now.

One Thing

I dreamed about Ireland,
and chocolate cake,
and a rescue wolf named Miles
whose fur was soft as rabbit fur.
I dreamed it was snowing,
fat, heavy flakes,
and I thought I would make pancakes for supper.

I slept under my owl comforter,
hoping for word from you,
but what I got instead
was a dream about a road trip
with Zen and Amy and Angel,
and it was early morning dark
when we stopped at a convenience mart
for doughnuts and caffeine
and discovered we had gone the wrong way
because I was the only one
who could read a map,
and I was sleeping.

Zen and I talked about San Miguel
and I told her about you,
the way I held your unresponsive hand
when they pulled the ventilator,
and you were gone without
once looking back.
She told me to call your mother, Hope.

When I woke up,
none of these things was true,
not Ireland nor the chocolate cake,
or the wolf and the snow,
but one thing is still bitter fact.
You are still gone.

No Reason

There's no reason
to get up this morning.
No reason not to,
except the mild inertia
of the warm coverlet,
the slight headache,
the press of the dog along your hip.

You set the table,
two plates, two forks, two knives,
the napkins lined up on the right side of each plate.
No reason not to.
Then you put one of each item away,
unused.

The tulips on the kitchen table are fading.
One petal plops down with a faint sound
like a door closing
in another part of the house.
Another follows.
By tomorrow morning,
you'll have nothing in the vase
but stems and stamens.
No reason not to tidy it up now,
put the spent flowers in the compost heap,
rinse out your grandmother's vase
and put it back in the hutch
with the wine glasses
and the brandy snifters
and the blue glass collection.

That compost, now,
it will make good tulips next spring.
No reason to think you might see them.
No reason not to.

Deep Love

for Hazel Hutchinson

It's a blessing
to spend better than sixty years
with the same man,
the deep love
that keeps your feet
rooted to this
piece of prairie,
lets your own roots
mingle with those of the buffalo grass,
the little bluestem.
He kept you anchored,
made you laugh,
carried you through darkness
when you thought you'd given up.
Now, he slips away in his sleep
like a memory.
You feel cut loose,
adrift, like a rowboat
untethered on the pond.
You feel as if you might
fly away,
drift into the sky
like the clouds that scud across
this April sky.
Your days lose structure.
Your nights are endless—
if you do sleep,
you wake at the sensation
of his hand on your back.
The dog whimpers in her sleep,
grieving too,
without understanding,
without hope.
You drift through

the first few days,
the funeral and the burial.
You lose most of the summer,
weeds rampaging
through the garden plot
you've always tended
so carefully.
It doesn't seem to matter.
Who will eat the canned tomatoes,
the green beans,
the potatoes and the carrots
that used to complement
so well the Sunday pot roast?
The dog is worried.
She brings you a Milkbone,
drops her head to her paws
when you absentmindedly stick it
into your pocket
instead of munching it up
as she'd intended.
It always makes her feel better.
So one day in early autumn,
the geese skeining across the sky,
the starlings filling the air
in a great restless flock,
you feel the stir,
the pull of the prairie,
the rootedness.
Walking out to the back pasture,
the dog gamboling at your heels,
you reach out, reach down, reach up,
feel the deep love,
know nothing
is ever lost for good.

At Least

My mind is too full for sleep
and the dog needs his midnight walk.
The world glitters with ice under the full moon
just moving into Virgo. The lunar guide says
this is the time to plant hedgerows,
to transplant old trees,
to weed and grapple with pests.

My thoughts are pests, stealing sleep.
The litany of if-onlys
replaced by small blessings—
at least he won't suffer the depredations
of Alzheimer's disease—
he won't forget my name or why I matter.
At least he won't get Parkinson's disease,
which he feared, with its hallucinations
and slow theft of self.
At least he never had to get that hearing aid
or teach another online class.
At least he got to see our puppy—he was
so proud of that dog—now full sized.
At least we got that new mattress.
At least I gave him his new anniversary bathrobe,
blue as the sky at dusk and warm and cozy,
to wear for his final ambulance ride to the Covid ward.
At least Biden won the election, and Kamala,
and at least he got to see it.
At least he knew I loved him,
even when we bickered.
At least he was happy.
At least we went to California last year
and wet our feet in the ocean.
At least he lived well and left a legacy of love.

At least when I go out tonight, wearing my
layers of down vest and coat, wool scarf,
wearing his warmest wool socks,
I'll see the stars and planets he loved to show me.
I'll look up at Orion
(I'll wear my distance glasses
so all is crisp
as a ringing bell)
and I will see the Seven Sisters dancing.
At least I'll always have the stars.

Counting Keys

My mother and I
sort through boxes of keys
at the breakfast table.
She is looking for the key to time,
I to keys that mark
the wheel of the year
 as we turn to darkness,
to fallow time,
to rest and deep thought.

The clock whirs and
its pine cone pendulums jig
as it ticks away the seconds,
each second a tick of my heart,
each heartbeat a harbinger of
the next world, the one I
hover near at night
and in deep winter.

Making Ralston

First, get down the big four-quart pot.
Set the stool just right,
so you can reach the stove
and yet be free to gaze out the window
over the sink,
across the fields of sugar beet
to the endless prairie,
the mountains like a low cloudbank
on the far horizon.
You've already stoked the stove with wood,
but for making Ralston,
you prefer the steady gas flame
of your new combination Kalamazoo range.
You'll have to sit there awhile,
stirring, so the pot doesn't boil over.

Start with two-thirds of a cup of molasses.
Sorghum will do,
but Karo syrup is too sickly sweet.
Avoid it. It needs to be bitter,
dark, a reminder
that the sweet is hard-won.
Add one-third cup of whole milk
from the dairy cow in the barn.
Set aside the rest
to make ice cream
for after dinner.
As the molasses starts to thin,
add brown sugar and bitter chocolate,
a quarter pound of butter.
Your undreamt-of granddaughters
will someday rely on store-bought
sticks of butter, measuring cups,

a candy thermometer,
but you can eye the weight
without thinking twice.
Stir the mixture constantly.
If you get distracted,
say, by the sight of your
young husband striding
across the fields,
coming in for lunch,
the candy will foam up all over
your shiny new stove.
Keep stirring until
a spoonful dropped into a dish of water
forms a soft ball.
If the ball is hard and cracks,
you've cooked it too long—
although some people like it that way,
hard, easier to suck on than to chew.
Prepare the baking sheet
with a piece of waxed paper
and pour the liquid mass
out to cool. Add black walnuts
if you have some.
When it cools, break it into pieces
and wrap each one.
When George heads back to the fields after lunch,
he'll take a piece for his pocket,
pop one into his mouth.
His kiss will be bitter,
but it will hold you up till sundown.

Someday your granddaughters
will use Ralston as a test

to weed out the boys who aren't serious,
the ones who don't know
that sometimes,
the bitter is the sweet.

Recognition

Time

*I'll come and find you
when it's time.*
I'm sure you said that to me
when you were eighteen,
on your way to Majorca
and a whole world of wandering,
and I was three, in Illinois.
I turned 40 and
I was still waiting—
years of running after you,
always surprised when
I touched your shoulder
and the wrong man turned
and snarled in my face.

I'll come find you when it's time.
You sent me press releases,
not because you knew me, but
because sending them was your job,
and responding was mine.
We didn't know then
that it was part of the dance.
I didn't recognize you
as the one I waited for.
And when I was on the cusp of 50,
and you were on the very brink of age,
we finally turned and
saw one another.

I reached for your hand
and your eyes flashed in recognition.
*You said you'd come for me
when it was time,* I said,
and you answered,
Why did you make me wait so long?

Full Moon at Pin Oak

The full moon floats on the surface of Pin Oak Lake,
so radiant and luminous her sister in the sky
seems but a pale reflection.
We lay on the bank counting the constellations,
and it's only the touch of your hand on mine
that anchors me from flying into the black winter sky.

Longing

Here in the east, the sun has set,
while westward where you are,
he still shines on fields of wheat,
dances on green rivers.

Only the moon sees in to my window:
She blushes to see my yearning for you.
This river laps my toes as I wade by the shore.
May it carry my essence downstream to your bed.

Crossroads

Last night I dreamed of keys,
one to a writing desk
and one to our hotel room in Santa Fe,
where we have never been.
I dreamed about a little girl
and woke to a voice whispering, *Grandma, Grandma,*
over and over.
Last night I buried my head under the covers
and held my breath
until the dream stopped calling.

Today, I step out.
The dog is on her leash,
but she doesn't need it.
It's for me, tethering me
to her wild instinct,
keeping me from flying
into my head and missing
the sweet gum balls like ornaments
on the forest floor,
the bur acorns like little hats,
the sunlight warm on my back,
the bright green moss
growing right down and under the water,
and under the water my face,
peering back up,
watching the way the trees lace earth to sky,
the way the dog's eyes shine.

We go to the five-pointed crossroad
just over the Missouri line.
I know where three of the roads go;
the other two remain mystery.

The dog starts a rabbit,
whose flight leads us
to look up and find ourselves face to face
with a white-tailed deer,
whose flight makes us look up
to see a red-tailed hawk take wing,
whose flight makes us look up.

At the end of the day,
the dog and I lay by the fire.
We are tired,
our bones heavy with the day.
When I sleep,
I dream you are calling my name.
I get up and follow you.

The Feather

A perfect barn owl feather,
tucked into my wallet
until I could get it home—
I know it's against federal law
to possess it—given I'm not recognized
as a shaman—but
it makes me happy.
Can that be wrong?

Stopping for gas on the way home
a week or so later,
I open my wallet,
having forgot the feather
and its perfection—
and happiness too—
a gust of wind snatches it up,
it spirals just out of reach—
flies over the highway,
higher, higher,
catching a thermal like
the memory of a hawk's wing.
And it's gone, oh, gone.

The gas pump clunks off.
I return the handle to its holder,
my credit card to its case.
I drive home, park the car
by the barn. The robins
nested there this spring,
and I can see a perfect half circle
of turquoise shell. I leave it lie.
At night, I dream of flying.

I Am

I am the phoenix.
I am the flame.
I am the grass growing over the graveyard,
and the star-shaped flowers
that spring forth in April.
I am all the world's oceans
reflected in a puddle of rainwater
by the barn behind the house
where I grew up.

I am the dairy cow and the river
and the oak tree and the wild grapevine,
the amoeba and the mastodon,
the bear, a salmon leaping from the water.
I am the smile on my dog's face,
the heartbeat of a baby in the womb,
its mother's milk.

I am the drummer and the drum.
I am a snow leopard
slinking, invisible, across the tundra.
I am the lichen and the moss.
I creep everywhere. I am eternal.
I am the phoenix and the flame.
I am the sky.

Return

Ragtop Down

They told me I was dying,
so I bought a red convertible
and started driving west
with the ragtop down,
the wind whipping over
my chemo-shorn skull,
and I sang,
I want to live,
I want to live,
I want to live in this beautiful world.

They cut off my breasts—
scooped out each and every last
malignant cell they could find.
I tattooed stars
where my nipples used to be.

But I have the BRCA-1 gene, and
the cancer settled in my right eye,
the good one, where I carry
my dreams and visions.
They said I'd go blind.
Hey, at least it cured my stigmatism.
I opened my two eyes wide
to take in the whole, from far horizon
right down to the smallest petal
of this one last spring,
and I sang,
I want to live,
I want to live,
I want to live in this beautiful world.

Then my kidneys failed.
They said I'd be on dialysis
for the rest of my suddenly foreshortened life
unless I found a donor—soon.
I tattooed a phoenix
rising up my spine
and I sang,
I want to live,
I want to live,
I want to live in this beautiful world.

I bought a turquoise leather fringed halter top vest
and stuffed the empty bosom
with flamboyant strands
of multicolored yarn.
I drove across the prairie
with my ragtop down,
the wind whipping over
my chemo-shorn skull.
I said, I am so beautiful.
I am so full of joy.
And I sang,
I want to live,
I want to live,
I want to live in this beautiful world.

And then—oh, then—
the Pandemic.
They carried my husband off
in an ambulance
and I never saw his smile again.
Garbed in full plastic protection,
I held his hand while they

pulled the ventilator,
his face ravaged, swollen,
gangrened.
He didn't respond. He slipped away.
It set me back—
I buried my face in the fall leaves
and sobbed.
It's easier to leave than to be left,
and my bones ached to just let go.
But I want to live.
I want to live.
I want to live in this beautiful world.

I got in my red convertible
and I drove west,
wind whipping over my chemo-shorn skull,
my husband's ashes in a velvet bag by my feet.
We scattered them over the indigo water of the bay,
as he'd asked,
and we cried and we sang,
and later that night,
I stood at the edge of the world,
my feet planted in the cold sand of Bolinas Beach.
I watched the waves,
saw the moon rise,
counted the stars,
picked up a piece of agate,
and I thought, I am so alone.
But I sang,
I am alive.
I am alive.
I'm still alive
In this beautiful world.

The Love Came Tumbling Down

So much sorrow—
a baby, dead in your arms,
that you might have saved
in your NICU in the States,
but not on this remote island
where a helicopter ride
to the war-torn mainland
costs a family's life savings.

The weeping mother
reaches for the tiny corpse,
her grim husband, helpless,
stroking her hair as she wails.

But also joy—
two children who were saved,
carried to the big hospital
through the stateside efforts
of your medical mission.

Home at last,
weary to the marrow,
you hang your jacket
in the front closet,
flick a switch,
step into your clean, bright
American living room.
Even though it's late,
why not?

Even though you can flip another switch
for free play,
you slip a quarter in the slot of the vintage jukebox,
push D1,
your favorite song,

watch the 45s
shuffle their way around,
drop into place,
the needle sliding
over the dead zone
and the first notes
echoing from your Rockhold speakers—

You remember a guest
in town for dialysis
waiting for a donor
to offer up a healthy kidney,
smiling, as you do,
in the face of Death.

The two of you,
strangers,
danced in the kitchen,
Wilson Pickett wailing,
I'm gonna wait
'til the midnight hour.

Your mind floats back
to Honduras,
the baby,
the weeping mother—
and maybe for a second
you wonder why
you do it
when it would be so easy
just to dance—

and then the love
comes tumbling down.

Rituals

We walked down to the river.
Becky was there in a folding chair,
and I sat on a mattress at her feet.
The mattress had been pulled from the RV—
she said, *You're welcome to sleep on it,*
if Mother will let you.

I said, *Oh, your mother!*
She stands at the foot of the bed
with such a baleful glare—then I say,
Becky said I could sleep here,
and she says, *Oh, my daughter.*
Tell her to be well. And disappears
before I can tell her they are both dead.

Your mother was a strong woman,
says Steve from the band,
lounging on his side across from us.
He is wearing a cap woven
by the hippie woman from Arcadia.
We are all masked against the Covid—
his has full curly goat horns,
Becky's has a monkey's face,
her own eyes bright and merry
behind the too-big eyeholes.
Kelli's mask is peacock feathers,
with a shimmering veil over her nose and lips.
She hums a descant while we talk.

I'm sorry you can't come to the ceremony,
I tell Steve.
Oh, we might, he says, *if*
the wind doesn't blow too hard.

If enough people come, I say,
we can do more rituals—
the coming of age ritual, and
one for going out. We can
do the evening ritual of
sitting around the fire singing,
and at dawn, the ritual
of welcoming the sun as it burns away
the mist and sets the river glowing
like a ribbon of flame.

Skiving Down the Bones

It's about the keenness of the blade,
honed to the sharp edge of a desert shadow.
It's about the angle of the cut.
Skiving the bones, I slice through accretions
of illness, the ash of chemo—
like stones, bones are hard to burn,
although you can break them
easily enough.

Skiving, I slice through layers of
loss and sorrow, honing in on what matters—
I quit worrying who will inherit my grandmother's china,
where my ashes will be dispersed.
Instead, I sharpen my skiving knife,
pressing metal blade to oiled whetstone.
All that's left is smooth, clean bone,
the fundament, the foundation,
the marrow that holds my DNA,
that tells the story of who I am.
I fold soft leather over this structure.
I fold my flesh
over my damaged, scarred bones.
I sew myself together.

Walking in Arcadia

For Nikki Patrick

Oh, Nikki—how nice to see you
wandering in the woods at Arcadia—
not that Arcadia, the one in Kansas—
although you looked so good
I had to work at remembering you are dead.

Your lovely long white hair was back to waist length.
You strode, no more shuffling with the walker
like the last time I saw you.

You were ranting about
the stupidity of people and their trash,
but you smiled when you saw me,
and you waited for me to join you.

The squirrels and birds followed you;
a fat raccoon chittered at your side,
no doubt regaling you about the family you fed
with cat food in the Before Time on Olive Street.
Rabbits darted away at my approach, and
a fat honeybee settled on your shoulder.

At first I thought you cut your hair, you said,
But you didn't, did you?
It's just growing back after chemo.
Nope, I cut it, I said. Remission.

And—I got my kidney transplant
Two weeks ago! You beamed—no other word for it—
asked, *Can I see your scar?*
and watched with macabre glee
and traced the staples
over my flank and down into my pelvis.

I'm so glad, you said simply.
I thought about suggesting you write an article about it,
but remembered you probably don't do that anymore.

I left you in the woods at Arcadia
and stepped back into the world,
new-made and healing.

Sound Healing

Lastacia strokes the singing bowls,
caresses the big gong and then
chimes the small one.
The rhythm settles my heartbeat.
The drum circle calms my deepest dread.

Tone and bass,
tone and bass,
heel and palm,
heel and palm,
the goatskin
thrumming under my fingertips,
vibrating up into my core,
my heart chakra.

This is my church.
This is my prayer.

After the third surgery,
after the chemo and
the deadly round of radiation,
I run my fingers
over my smooth plastic breasts,
the tattooed garden hiding
the missing nubs that used to sing
under your fingertips,
your hands thrumming across my torso,
heel and palm,
tone and bass, tone and bass,
stroking just below my ribs.

You are my church, oh, lover.
This is my prayer.
Oh, pray for me.
Pray for me.

Moon Watcher

Moon watcher, mother, meticulous balancer,
her shining light has always
lit my path from behind,
even when clouds occluded it,
my way lost like an asteroid
adrift in a galaxy of fixed globes,
pinballing wildly.

Tonight, the moon is dark,
the sky an endless soft expanse
of black, only a couple of faint stars—
the winter constellations making way for summer's.
We're walking the dogs—
there have always been dogs, too.
She carries the flashlight,
I hold the leashes.
We count each star;
the dogs count every bush and shrub.
We cast our circle
over the sleeping neighborhood,
lock the gates,
put out the lights.

A Certain Kind of Alchemy

To take a pinch of this
and a dab of that
and end by spreading dinner on the table.

To raise the sourdough mother,
caring for it like a little manikin,
feeding it until it bubbles happily,
tending it until a sweet, tangy pinch
becomes a loaf of bread
you spread with butter and homemade jam.

To survive an illness that almost kills you,
the kind where the treatment
is as devastating as the disease,
and come out on the other side
the person you were always meant to be,
all pretensions burned away by chemo,
and only truth remaining.

Just to wake up in the morning
and enjoy the scent of rain in the air,
to be alive and grateful for it.

Publishing Credits

"Making Ralston," *Dead Housekeeping*, July 13, 2020.

"Oblivion Tango," *Wandering Bone,* Meadowlark Press: Emporia, 2017.

"A Woman is Walking," *Sisterspeak*, Summer 2016.

About the Author

Photo by Amy Nixon.

Olive L. Sullivan is the author of *Wandering Bone* (Meadowlark Press, 2017), a collection of travel poems. Her poetry has also appeared in several journals including *The Midwest Quarterly*, *The Little Balkans Review*, and the online magazine *Dead Housekeeping*, as well as in the award-winning anthology *Begin Again: 150 Kansas Poems*. She has published short fiction and creative essays and performs regularly with the band Amanita. She holds an MFA from Stonecoast at the University of Southern Maine and an MA from the University of Colorado-Denver. A bookbinder, she lives in Pittsburg, Kansas, where she grew up. She loves taking long walks on the prairie with dogs and traveling anywhere that requires a passport—and almost anywhere that doesn't.

Also by
Olive L. Sullivan

"With wildly original images, sparkling wit, and a voice all her
own, Olive writes poetry of expansive courage and vision,
tipping over the edge of dreams we can remember without
understanding, and celebrating the impermanence of life's
nuances. In the end, she illuminates the vital colors, textures,
shapes of pure desire, deep quandaries, and the kind of
exploration that brings us to the essence of home—all on the
way to "Welcome the spirits in." As she writes in her poem,
Praise Song for the River, "We come to god each in our own
way/ but we find ourselves on the banks of the same river,/ our
hot feet dangling in the same cool green water." This collection
of poetry shines with originality, wisdom, and power as it
continually tilts the reader toward new ways to perceive their
own journeys."

—Caryn Mirriam-Goldberg, 2009-13 Kansas Poet
Laureate, *How Time Moves: New and Selected Poems*

MEADOWLARK POETRY

Meadowlark

Books are a way to explore, connect, and discover. Poetry incites us to observe and think in new ways, bridging our understanding of the world with our artistic need to interact with, shape, and share it with others.

Publishing poetry is our way of saying—

We love these words,
we want to preserve them,
we want to play a role in sharing them
with the world.

Meadowlark Press
— since 2014 —

meadowlarkpoetrypress.com

www.ingramcontent.com/pod-product-compliance
Lightning Source LLC
Chambersburg PA
CBHW071104120626
46546CB00003B/1270